Zen Pig

Volume 2 / Issue 3

Feelings Are Clouds

written by:
mark brown

illustrated by:
anastasia khmelevska

each copy sold gives
1 person clean water
for 1 year

Come say "Hi!" to Zen Pig online:
ZenPigBook.com

Don't forget, Zen Pig loves seeing pictures of his new home and new friends -
#ZenPig on Instagram to send them his way!

-Dedicated to my mom-
who has faithfully journeyed with a servant's heart.

You have touched countless lives - I love you.

Another Autumn had come.
Brilliant leaves were raining down
On Zen Pig and the others
At the Farmers Market in town.

Zen Pig was enjoying every step
On the cool, crunchy ground.
But then he had to stop,
Because he heard a crying sound.

A familiar face, it was Zen Pig's niece,
Who had lost her father in the crowd.
"It's OK, climb on," he said
As he knelt with a bow.

Little Pig jumped right up,
She knew he'd help her find her way.
As they walked through the market,
She listened to what he had to say.

"Together, we will find your Dad,"
Zen Pig spoke with ease.
"We all lose our way sometimes,
In fact, even me.

When we're lost, we can feel things
Like sadness come around;
But know that it is normal,
There's no shame in feeling down.

Anger too will pay a visit
As you continue to journey on,
But know that its stay is short
And soon it will be gone.

At times, fear will cast a shadow
On your heart and on your mind,
Just count your breaths, in and out,
And then your light will shine.

Remember what these feelings are,
Simply rolling clouds in the sky,
Blocking for just a moment
The light you have inside.

Your true nature is your joy
Behind the clouds it beams.
Take comfort, your light is always there,
Even when it cannot be seen."

Atop Zen Pig's shoulders,
Little Pig could see so much more.
Even though she had gotten lost,
She had found what she was looking for

Just then, her dad was spotted,
With love they came together,
But now she knew she could shine,
No matter what the weather.

Namaste.

("The light in me loves the light in you.")

_____'s Zen Pig Collection

☐ Zen Pig

☐ The Wonder We Are

☐ All That Is Needed

☐ Where You'll Find Love

☐ Here to Do

☐ Feelings Are Clouds

It's hard to believe that even today, so many still do not have access to clean water.

But YOU are helping.

Digging new wells, building fences to keep livestock from contaminating sources, repairing existing wells, and constructing toilet slabs give much needed help to communities in need.

Thank You.

What feelings visited you today?